W9-BVS-940

DAY BY DAY

Illustrated by John A. Penrose

DEANE BUTLER EDWARDS

day by day

HERALD PUBLISHING HOUSE
Independence, Missouri

Copyright © 1965

HERALD PUBLISHING HOUSE

INDEPENDENCE, MISSOURI

Library of Congress
Catalog Card No. 65-26288

Printed in the United States of America

DEDICATED

to

Pebble, Caryl, Frances

PREFACE

To Deane Edwards, life itself is a gift to be grateful for, and to be savored. No little happiness is too small to escape her awareness. No catch of pain within the soul of a fellow wayfarer is hidden from her sensitive perception. So it is that, within these common poems of every day, there threads an uncommon keenness of vision, a humble sharing of the rich, though sometimes small, treasures, the little laughters, which life offers to all of us, but which appear to each of us in different fashion, against the backdrop of the path we alone have chosen among the thousand paths of living.

LOUISE SCOTT WRIGLEY

ACKNOWLEDGMENTS

I am grateful to Paul Wellington, managing editor at Herald House, who understood the need for polishing these poems for publication. He aided me in gaining criticism that pointed toward a proper approach to revision.

Louise Wrigley again lent her talent and gently criticized the final drafts. I find it difficult to properly thank her, but she will understand.

DEANE EDWARDS

SECTION I
POEMS OF PHILOSOPHY

THE SEARCH

Sometimes, I feel the stars so near
That I can clutch one from the sky;
That there was never day, nor year,
Nor anyone, not even I
Apart from universal whole;
A perfect plan with all control
Led onward by creative hand
That has forever known and planned.

I feel that time can breathe no more,
My hand against a firm closed door
That hinge-locked will not let me hence;
But, holds me fast within the veil
Of animated life-suspense.
Sometime, I shall prevail!

That door shall then be opened wide,
And I shall step at last inside.
All truth will be revealed to me,
And I shall ever more be free.
To know! When shall I worthy be?
In Life? In Death?
In Immortality?

12

TRANSIENT

If I had never watched an ocean roll,
Beheld majestic mountain peaked with snow,
Or smelled magnolias opened by the rain,
I would now vouch that living was in vain
When all of nature dead about me lies;
Nor dares to reach her withered, thirsting eyes
Upward to the blistering, sun-scorched skies.

I yearn to take my flight once more,
Like migrant bird with ancient moorings soar,
To come to rest upon a sand-soft shore,
Sighting sails skimming on a landless sea;
To know again that vast and lovely schemes
Lie far beyond the little world of Me.

KINSHIP

To everyone the wise man knows
Must come great sorrow. So he grows.
Remember when your cross you face,
Beside you walks the human race!

OZARK HOME

I have heard the ocean rush and roar
　　With foaming lips,
Tired from its rolling, ageless trips
　　From shore to shore;
Smelled magnolias opening in the rain
　　In southern spring.
Viewed mountains high by soft clouds paled
　　White-capped above,
Like heads of regal ladies, breathless, veiled
　　Before they love.

I have often seen the timid fawn
　　Pause at dawn,
As Red Coat Mounty brushed through woody
　　　trail;
　　Felt heart fail,
Lest I betray a soft and gentle eye
　　To gun nearby,
Waiting there to still a heart and brain
　　With rifle rain;
Breathing deep the pine and fir tree smell
　　The winds propel.

14

Pityingly I saw the beggar dive
    On foreign strand,
Grinning, toothless, raise his dripping hand
    To prove alive;
Laughing, half from gain—and half in fear
    With shark so near—
    Eager more for bread
Than for ribbed body frail, half-clothed, half-
    fed;
    His teeth destroyed
To hold in mouth the coin from watery void.

I came home to my deciduous trees
    Brushed by breeze;
With lace-like leaves held against the moon
    Hiding coon;
To shimmering trout in pebbled, rippling stream
    That moving gleam;
To dogwood, pink and white against the hill.
    My heart was still.

Here I belong as an adopted child
    With parent mild;
Clinging closer to a mother's hand—
    The Chosen Land!

RACE EXTENDED

Now, I say complacently,
"I remember ten years back,"
As though it was just recently.
Of time I often just lose track!

I listen to still older ones
With talk of fifty years ago.
They wonder how to tell their sons
That years go rolling fast not slow.

A philosophic thought must come
As life goes rushing through; we see
That we are only in one run
Of all the race life is to be.

ETERNAL RHYTHM

Suddenly we all break forth
Like rushing waters from a dam
    Too long pent up.
Crumbling walls respond to pressure's ram,
Growing pulse of atoms and the things
    That make up brains!

The pressure comes, but where and why?
This ultimate of life and rhythm,
    The basic cry!

Electrons circling apex round;
In sinewed muscles flexing, flexing,
    As they run;
In turning earth around the sun;
Multitudinous vibrations struck
    Sound link on link.
Or thoughts, connected as we think,
Reach at last the cresting brink
    Fill and spill.
We breathe, we sleep, we work, we eat
Accompanied by the pulsing beat
    Of faithful heart.

What is this pulse apparent?
Can this be love inherent—
    The heart of God?

17

NATURE'S GEOMETRY

There is a kind of symmetry
That nature calls her very own;
A graceful femininity
Even in the way a stone
May press against the friendly ground;
In curve of fallen twig and branch
Rotten, brittle all around.

There is the misty mood of moon
On rows and rows of jagged trees,
Above the ribboned river lagoon;
Dead stillness without midnight breeze.
Eroded earth at water's edge
From fertile fields the stolen dredge.

Ethereal, casual the advances,
Nature's own, her touch enchances.

18

LOSS

I see your shoes sitting there,
Shining bright, ready to wear.
I know a war has taken your soul
And I am as dead—
    as much as though
It had taken mine.

How can they shine?

SILENT YIELDINGS

I planted ninety tulips.
The leaves are cutting through.
Rows of yellow jonquils;
Crocus gold and blue.

Of all I'd rather do
From day to day, I know,
Is watch green things heave through
To end the time of snow.

THE TREE PLANTER

I set a sturdy oak in soil and sand.
Its gnarled fingers like a toiler's hand
Firm and strong for stolid years will stand.

The willow, by a fountain's splashing flow,
Its slender fingers bending long and low,
Reminds of southern climes, and long ago.

This elm shall guard my grandchild's play,
Above his laughing glee at day.
Its lacy branches will in moonlight sway.

Though I shall die, so glad am I to see
The vistas of a future time to be.
So simply wrought, this joy—to plant a tree.

"LET THERE BE LIGHT!"

The old year's gone!
Come New Year's dawn!
Vintage, joy and sorrow,
Tests to shape tomorrow!

Life is like the seasons old,
Patterned portraits, artful, bold.
Spring with flowering love bedecked;
Youth soon flees to retrospect.

Summer storms with lightning flecked,
Glaring flash to greet our sight,
With truth that shines too bright
As yet, for us to understand
That first and mighty God-command!

Fall, half-gay, so short and fleeting,
Somber, sad her fateful greeting.
Wistful gladness stirs the heart;
We feel a plan; we see but part.

When winter comes, the truth we know.
We quiver in the northwind blow;
That makes the end as white as when
We face, at last, the time of snow!

PURPOSE

Intensity in all we meet;
In household work and chores;
In keeping children daily neat;
In washing, scrubbing floors.

In laughter yet unfeigned and real;
In sorrow's ache or throbbing feel;
In silence, still and very sweet—
With vibrant loneliness replete;
Returning us, renewed with grace,
To join again the human race.

FINAL FRIENDS

The last decade of my life
I'll spend among good books.
Away from worry, fear, and strife,
I'll search the hidden nooks
Of all the great minds that have been.
So, when I die, I will not fear,
Though death comes with a deafening din,
For truth I'll know so very near!

ACCEPTANCE

What have you done for me, love?
Beyond the laughter of a friend;
Beyond the smile of neighbor near;
Of childish laughter tinkling clear.

Beyond the grateful widow's tear;
Beyond the praise that men will lend;
Or intent intellect I know
Opening wonder-realms below.

You have laughed my faults away,
Made them nothing left to prey;
Granted charity for fear;
Loved me as I am, my dear!

Why God, for me, has made it so
I cannot fathom, only know.
So laud benevolence above,
Because He gave me you, love!

LOVE REGAINED

I held my love with tight-closed hand
So from my grasp it could not flee.
I felt it slip my fingers like the sand,
Slowly sifting out from me.

I find my wound, though scarred, is healed.
A different life is now revealed.
My hand lies open, resting love so free;
Nor does it move to go away from me.

WHENCE THE SPIRIT?

I listened long to what the preacher said
As noble thoughts went racing through my head.
A brilliant mind he surely has, I thought,
As golden words from out his mouth were
    wrought.

To walk anew I find I cannot start;
There's nothing really changed within my heart!

24

JUSTICE

We cheat the law of averages
For days, perhaps, for years.
We act like social savages,
Pretend we have no gnawing fears
Of losing money, friends, or hope;
But in the end we cannot cope
With universal law, whose scope
Binds the whole of us in sway.
We each but have our little day.

Then the tide is turned to flow
Like rushing waters, maybe, slow,
Depending on the things we sow.
Perhaps, to drown, or thirst to quench.
By moral law we are entrenched!

Some call it fate, we to sorrow bow;
Some call it punishment for sin;
Yet, we must surely feel somehow,
Though sore the test as on we plod,
Faced test brings closeness to our God.
And as we love from day to day
That love comes back to us to pay
The debt for mercy that is great.

Count me no follower of fate!

TO A WORKMAN

I saw the sun go down last night,
    Casting light
With ray-like tendrils through the snow,
    A crimson glow.
Above the church tower, spiraled cross—
    Gold-embossed.

I saw a workman's silhouette
    Against sunset,
Battered dinner pail a-swinging.
Just then from out the heavenly glow,
    I know,
I heard celestial choirs singing!

LOVE'S EMPATHY

When I see a small hungry child,
Hungry for love and for bread;
When I see a forgotten old man
Watching time pass without dread;
When I see mankind yearn to be free
Knowing within they may never be,
I wonder how God feels, seeing it all,
Who loves each bird as He watches it fall!

MATURATION

What whispering, chilled, perspiring fear
Chides man to this neurotic waste?
Where all seem in a maddening, stumbling haste
To run the gauntlet, as machines propelled;
To fall in rows as trees by woodman felled.

We cannot wait for pleasure's ripening year,
But pick its coming fruit
Yet green with bitterness,
Without the benefit of browning rays
That friendship, love, and truth make suit,
Long-lived in lighted, seasoning days.

THE GENTLE FOLK

Thank God for all the gentle folk
Whose life-raw hearts forever yearn
To comfort and be comforted;
Always feel within them burn
The light of truth—yet, half-aware,
Half-knowingly each comes
With pent-up power of loving born,
Which in his burdened bosom drums!

So capable of anything—
Of making ancients yet to sing;
Of teaching children how to grow;
Of making wise men further know
Of purpose far beyond their ken.
These crawled the hills with bleeding skin.

Oh, love of God that dwells within,
Make me meek and part of them!

CONSCIENCE

The tension wire of living was yet taut.
His step, though slow and meditative, sure.
He'd bowed in battle; yet, he bravely fought
For truth so pure!

A joy he found on battlefield that day
In self-respect; so, went upon his way
Unscarred by loss, or crowned by victory.
Oh, how I wish that I had known the loss,
And he were me!

INNOCENCE

A wise man philosophically has said,
"Of all the glories of this world to know
Is he who suffers long with unbowed head;
Nor to those near him of his sorrow show."

True, from pain our character may grow;
Still, sometimes I yet yearn to see
The unscathed innocent—so gay, so free!

RECOMPENSE EARNED

Today I make this solemn resolution
Though my throbbing problems need solution,
To ease my mind of sickening, aching pain;
I'll never stir still waters just to gain
    Peace for myself.

Now I see why older folk have learned
To live their lives becalmed from day to day,
Rewarded only for the things they've earned
Leagues behind on their unchartered way.

Never was a man appreciated
Who forced his worth upon another's mind;
Nor can pain ever be alleviated
Except through constant effort to be kind.

30

TEARS

These tears in youth we come to know
Cool, refreshing, rimming slow,
Of joy that calms our deadening fear
As children's anchoring hands pull near.

Warm tears for natural loss of friend,
Or when our hearts to others lend,
In empathetic, beating pain,
Having felt the throb again.

Hot tears of doleful, dark despair,
Like blood from dying heart is wrung
After love with joy has blended.
The song of youth has just been ended.

So, age is but the end of tears;
The wellspring being, spent with years,
Left shriveled flesh,
No fountain flow
Of joy
Of love
Of grief we know.

MUSIC INHERENT

My parents say of noble blood I come.
Blue blood I have, if not a lot, well, some.
I wonder then when I hear rhumba drum
I feel as though I must go wild and free!
Can this be my ancestry down in me?

Hungarian music on a violin
Brings gnawing, throbbing hunger from within.
My heart is drawn with strings, thread-fine, web-
    thin.
My soul is never full of hearing sound
Of violins like human tongues unbound.

Mozart and Bach, Beethoven, Schumann, Brahms,
Affect me all, as peace proclaiming psalms.
They take me from the realms of finite qualms.
Can such emotion really stem from me,
With all that I'm supposed in me to be?

32

I think . . .
A gypsy my great-grandpère was so free!
My great-grandmère from southern clime was
    she.
They taught their children laughter, love, and
    glee;
And though this side in hue is not so blue,
I like this mongrel part the best, don't you?

LOVE OF GOD

Love of God, who can tell?
Who can fathom that great well?

Ever present, ever new,
Linking earth with heaven, too.

All gone by, all to come;
Unseen by most, glimpsed by some.

Love of God, unchanged and true,
Finite to infinite, lift us to you!

MY FRIEND HAS FALLEN

Beat the drum,
Play the fife!
Make me feel,
"War is life!"

Beat the fanfare!
(Shrewd men counsel—
Arm unbare)
Make music swell!
Let me one moment
Forget this hell!

Tomorrow's sun can never rise
Again so glorious before my eyes.

CREATION'S PAIN

What toil there is for us to sow
A simple, yellow jonquil row.
And, oh, the after-work we know
When tiny seeds we chance to grow.

How often in the still of night
I see an artist by his light;
Or hear the silence broken by
A newborn child or mother's cry.

Why is it so that all we know
Of value here to gain
Must scar our hands with toil below,
Be born in labor's pain?

And as I dwell upon this thought
I think of God!
What He has wrought!

FAITH, KNOWLEDGE, FAITH

Much knowledge often brings to one a kind of
      skepticism.
We see man as he goes along as just an organism,
Today, pulled-puppet on a string; tomorrow gone,
While all the universe rolls on, and on,
      And on, and on.

As we learn what wondrous powers of universe
      decree,
Why is it, then, so difficult for you and me to see
That man is surely, also, free—unbound by Earth
      or Mars,
And has a future longer, greater, than the bright-
      est stars!

Section II
Poems about Children

YOUTH CAMP

Off-to-camp excitement—
Shoes, boxes, dreams.
What an awful frightment!
Blouses, scissors, creams.

One for the hair;
One for the skin;
One for the eyebrows—
"Aren't mine too thin?"

"Where's my guitar?
Want to learn how to chord.
Move your foot over,
Can't touch the floorboard!"

All the things loaded,
Can't see out to drive.
The back wheel springs
Will never survive!

We've lost little Frances.
Where can she be?
Stuffed in the corner
Like a piece of debris!

There goes the radio,
The Beatles are on.
"For heaven sakes,
What is that song?!"

Everyone is in,
"Don't anyone get lost."
One false move
And it's holocaust!

"Watch out, Pebble,
That's the footfeed.
Don't be a rebel,
Speed we don't need."

Small, quiet Caryl
Sitting by the door,
Watching the action;
She thinks it's a bore.

Sweatshirts and jeans—
All poking out;
The bulge of the bags
Leaves one in doubt!

Clean smell of hair,
Every head washed,
Even if each
Seems slightly squashed.

Look at all three.
Each meets my eye.
"Can't they stay home?"
I'm going to cry!

EXPERIENCE

I studied child psychology
And my expoundings were not mild.
I think it all mythology
Since rearing now an only child!

CHILD PSYCHOLOGY?

The babe has learned psychology
At this most tender age of three.
When we scold her for a muss,
She first makes just an awful fuss,
Then cries and pleads with woeful face.
She leads us quite a merry chase.
When none of this works out so well,
With charming way she casts her spell;
Apologizing then so sweet,
She wins again the ruler's seat!

REPENTANCE

A broken tulip on the floor—
I scolded, angry-hearted!
I wish she'd picked a dozen more
To dry the tears I started!

TEEN-AGERS

We have teen-agers,
Three to be exact.
How we survive
Is an unknown fact!

From dawn till dark
And 'way after that
We whirl and we swirl.
At last I park,
Back down flat.
"What's that in my bed?"
A bristly hair roller
From someone's head!

Car's never there;
Phone always busy;
Leaves our daddy
In an awful tizzy!
"How can I call you?
Get another phone!
Or better still,
Let's just leave home!"

"Mamma, do something
With this awful hair!
Sally's hair's curly.
It's just not fair!"
"How many calories
Are on this plate?
Never, never, never
Am I going to gain weight!"

"Help me with these formulas,
I know I'll fail!
On second thought,
Can I go with Gail?
Two study periods
Should get me ready.
Say, did you know,
Jane's going steady?"

Three lie sleeping
Deep in warm beds;
Big hair rollers
On weary little heads.
When they are gone,
What will I do?
Desolate my heart
Till they're home anew!

GRACELAND INITIATION

We are the little scummsies,
When spoken to, we runnsies.
It isn't any funnsies,
To be such little dumbsies!

When all the men do sees us,
They run behind the treesus.
Of course, our looks don't please us
When all the fellows leaves us!

Actives some day you'll find us,
And then we'll leave behind us
The curse which now does bind us:
The art of "How to mind us!"

BINDING

I watched our babe wash her hands;
The soap she clutched quite tight to hold.
Those tiny fingers, too, enfold
My heart . . .
Like tight-pulled bands.

LOOSENING

One-half the time is nearly gone
When I can have you all alone,
And watch your baby hands hold on
To toys and things that are your own.

Then off to school all gay you'll go!
And I, my dear? I'll cry.
Some day you'll do the same I know;
Some day you'll see the reason why.

NOSTALGIA, THREE TIMES OVER

FIRST BABY

Tiny feet I hear
Patting all day long.
Nothing quite so dear
As their little song!

SECOND BABY

Why is it when you're sound asleep, my babe,
After a day with laughs and tears and play,
I want to wake you up and see you smile,
Though you have slept for such a little while?

THIRD BABY

Little girl's toys strewn on the floor,
Broken, worn shoes from days of yore,
Gone from sight forever more;
Yet, memory holds each part so near
Within my pulsing heart, my dear!

CONSISTENCY

Among the more familiar things
About our house we hear the most,
Each morning as the school bell rings,
Are sounds of scraping well-burned toast!

UNLIKELY BONUS

Diapers to hang;
Ironing to do;
Doors going bang!
"Please, tie my shoe!"
So goes my day,
Nighttime, too.
With one hour of play,
What would I do!

DOGGY PREFERENCE

Two "Bow-Wows" our babe has now
To run with her each merry day.
I wish someone would tell me how
They stand her rough-and-tumble play.
She yanks and pulls their long, black ears,
Dumps water in their meaty food.
They seem to have no doggy fears,
Though she is most unusually rude.

I watch them fight from dawn till night
And find it difficult to see
Why they prefer her over me!

AGENCY STOLEN

I saw a wreck today.
A little boy was dead!

What fools we are to play
With childish lives and laughter.
We leave them not to say
What tragedy comes after!

TO A CHILD

Our babe lies in her trundle bed
A-talking all the thoughts
That, passing through her golden head,
Seem most delightful to her ear!
Of toys, of trains, of people dear.

Of ugly things she has no fear;
All things to her in beauty grow.

A child's the closest thing to God
I know!

SECTION III
POEMS
OF
THIS
AND
THAT

The cat's asleep beside the fire;
The lights are burning low.
The beating of a hurried heart
Is growing slow on slow.

I dream then, for a little while,
Of things that in past years
Made me happy, and I smile
At childish laughs and fears.

In rushing, oblique, racing dreams
I look for future things to come.
Of all my well-laid plans and schemes,
I hope I realize just one!

The days aren't long enough, it seems,
To work, and play, and make my dreams.
I have to take up 'most the night.
—I save the dreams for candlelight.

I am so tired when I arise
I wish, sometime, I would be wise,
And go to bed while it's still night.
Instead, I read till morning bright
Fills my windowpane with light.

The hours I keep, I must admit
For being human—just don't fit.

~◦◦~

When I was kind to someone,
I thought I saw her frown.
Today she brought me strawberries
When she came into town.

~◦◦~

Our train got stalled; six hours we lolled,
And talked and laughed and had a sing.
In trouble all in all confide.
It's then we learn a hopeful thing:
We're all alike 'way down inside.

THE UNEXPLORED

I met a well-known lady
Who does so many things;
She paints, collects, and gardens,
Even plays and sings!

I told her she was great;
She made me feel quite small.
She only smiled and said,
"Talent sleeps in us all!"

~ 9c ~

I'm back in the city on foot.
I watch the traffic as it flows
In endless rhythm, stops and goes.
I pause to wipe the smoky soot
That smears the end of my nose.

Bottles of medicine on the shelf,
All sizes and kinds, guardians of health.
Grim, jagged lines of soldiers true,
We've placed, too much, our trust in you!

When the house is an awful clutter
Friends call for one thing and another.
I wish, one time when we're shiny bright,
Just one of all would hit it right
Who came to call or visit me.

So sad it seems it cannot be!

I rush about from day to day;
I think, I'm really "making hay."
But when my bed and I have parted,
I'm back again just where I started!

I want to know,
When one dies
If all control
Leaves you; so
You cannot will
The Spirit's soul
More to rise
From out the sod,
Up to God?

Gentle Spirit,
In me singing,
"I shall be free!
To go a-winging
Like a bird;
To do the things
I think to me
That human ear
Has never heard!"

IMPERFECT RHYME —
IMPERFECT PEOPLE!

I think I'll quit the beauty shop;
It hurts my human vanity
To see my hair look like a mop
In unadorned reality!

I know I must diet;
I just can't deny it.
Why should fate have picked me
To broaden so quickly?

The world is so big, and I am so small;
Seems I'm really not much at all.
I think most folks must feel the same:
Wanting attention, love and fame,
'Cause if I'm just a little kind,
They tell me all that's on their mind!

I'm so tired, I'd like to sleep
The clock hands twice around.
But if I wasn't needed,
This truth I've always found:
Being unneeded makes me sad.

I guess when I am tired,
Down inside I'm glad!

When walking down a busy street,
A kindly face I chance to meet.
I want to stop someone so kind
To tell him what is on my mind.

My brand-new shoes are tight;
They just don't fit at all.
I'll wear them though, all right;
They make my foot look small!

I had an exuberant time
Talking to a friend of mine.
She let me talk about myself,
To brag, lament, and everything else.

To me a lady, helpful, kind.
But, now a question comes to mind.
The answer sure, I'd like to see;
What does she really think of *me?*

Someone left her hat
Where she sat,
Lying on a chair.
I'd as soon
Leave it there,
Friendly boon
Of sunny afternoon.

I had a sorrow once,
I feared I should die.
I lost it all
When once I saw
The lonely fears,
The unshed tears
In faces passing by.

How I recall when I was eight!
I thought I'd *never* get to nine!
My viewpoint's changed
    just here of late,
Birthdays could stop—
Especially *mine!*

Every time I start to write
My pen is always lost somewhere.
It grieves me just an awful sight,
So *many* feel I've one to spare!

I finished my book today;
I feel I have lost a friend.
I'm sad, in a wistful way,
To see those words, "The End."

This radio story each day
I wish would finally end;
Or, all their lives would mend;
Or, else just go away!

It doesn't hurt my egotism
To study Wells or Darwinism.
Though once a one-cell organism,
See the heights to which I've risen!

If people are not kind,
The thing I grieve to see
Is that I look to find
Unkindness down in me!

60

I like to be sensitive to each little thing,
To feel each moment with joy or with pain.
I know I shall wear out before it's my time,
But I shall have touched, sometime, the sublime!

I'm in an awful plight!
I have one poem to write.
I cannot make a start,
'Cause nothing's in my heart!

I wish when I do something nice
I'd let the doing just suffice;
But to the world I fairly shout it.
I find I'm awfully smug about it!

I saw someone I hardly knew.
She told me trouble she'd been through.
She listened too, seemed not to mind.
I have a new friend now, I find.

Early on these shivery morns
I pity all the working races—
Those who leave a spot so warm
To scurry out and wash their faces!

I find when I am "company"
I want to be alone.
I'd like to wander just as free
As when I am at home.

I don't know why I'm never gay.
I can't explain it quite away.
I guess, because I feel the strain
My hostess feels to entertain!

I see life come;
I see life go.
I wonder some,
Why it is so?

I hate to go to teas
To sit and look so pleased;
To chat about the snow;
Behind the back a word
To ever whisper low,
"Say, have you heard?" . . .
Or, "Did you know?" . . .

POEMS OF CHRISTMAS

If snowflakes fall on Christmas Day,
I'm never really very cold.
My heart's all warm and full of play,
And gentle blessings, hundredfold!

Of all the things I did in youth
That I am sorry for,
Was that bewildering Christmas Eve
I peeked from closet door.

Since then all things have changed for me;
I'll never ever be the same.
There underneath my Christmas tree
Was Santa Claus with father's name!

Christmas, enchanted time of the year—
Snowflakes glistening, holly rich and green;
Memories of childhood hovering near;
Young love laughing, gay on the scene;
Brilliant starred night with fields even laid
As on the night the shepherds prayed.

Christmas, most holy day of the year,
Teach me thy holiness—Love without fear!